IMAGES
of America

FOSS MARITIME
COMPANY

At the time this photograph was taken, Thea (1858–1927) and Andrew Foss (1855–1937) were able to smile at their accomplishments. They had transitioned two moves, one from Norway to the United States and a second from Minnesota to Tacoma, Washington. In Tacoma, they constructed a waterfront float home and started a rowboat and launch business. The couple watched with pride as their young children started to help develop what would become one of the largest tugboat companies in the world. (Courtesy Foss Maritime.)

ON THE COVER: Captain Sporman points to the famous four-masted schooner *Commodore*, which the *Arthur Foss* had just towed with 1.5 million board feet of lumber from Puget Sound mills to Los Angeles. During the voyage, the schooner's rigging was still usable, and the sails were raised to help make a quick weeklong voyage possible. (Courtesy Foss Maritime.)

IMAGES
of America

FOSS MARITIME COMPANY

Mike Stork

ARCADIA
PUBLISHING

Published by Arcadia Publishing
Charleston SC, Chicago IL, Portsmouth NH, San Francisco CA

Printed in the United States of America

Library of Congress Catalog Card Number: 2006938512

For all general information contact Arcadia Publishing at:
Telephone 843-853-2070
Fax 843-853-0044
E-mail sales@arcadiapublishing.com
For customer service and orders:
Toll-Free 1-888-313-2665

Visit us on the Internet at www.arcadiapublishing.com

To my family, my parents, Ed and Ebba Stork; my wife, Kathie; and children, Rachel and Jim

CONTENTS

ACKNOWLEDGMENTS

This book would have been impossible without the help of many Foss families, employees, retired boatmen, and customers. I must first thank Foss customer service manager and historian Mike Skalley. Mike opened the company archives for me and answered numerous questions. Dispatchers who have kept me abreast of Foss activities include John Lewis, Bert Wyant, Sandy Macham, Steve Spencer, Jim Crowley, Chris Wolf, Susan Dyer, Lloyd Wibur, and Don Hogue. Foss management who provided photo opportunities include Toby Holmes; Bruce Reed; Hap Richards; Scott Merritt; Matt Brown; John Barrett; Steve Kimmel; Don McElroy; Andy Stephens; Paul Gallagher, the world's best press boat FRV (Fast Response Vessel) driver; and *Tow Bitts* editor Bruce Sherman.

A warm thank you to all the captains and crews who have welcomed me aboard their tugs.

Great tugboat friends include Robin and Kae Patterson, Shawn and Mike O'Connor, Bud Hopkins, Boyd Galligan, Jay Peterson, Bert Homes, Norm Manly, and Mark Freeman.

Foss family members sharing stories and photographs include the late Drew Foss and Tooty Foss Hager, Peter Campbell, Duncan Campbell, Sandra Campbell Wright, Tina Foss, Diane Foss, Leslie Foss, Brynn Foss Rydell, and Shannon Bauhofer.

Museum and library staff includes Caroline Marr, Museum of History and Industry (MOHAI), and Karl House, Puget Sound Maritime Historical Society.

I am especially indebted to Brian Kamens and Robert Schuler of the Tacoma Public Library Northwest Room. Also generous in helping were Evette Mason, Port of Tacoma; Vicki Blackwell, Gig Harbor Peninsula Historical Society; Elaine Miller, Washington State Historical Society; and Ron Magden, Dale Wirsing, and Paul Michaels of the Tacoma Historical Society.

Heartfelt thanks to high school intern Holly Skewis and her father, Capt. Eric Skewis; filmmakers Nancy Haley and Lucy Ostrander; and Tom Cashman and Mary Bowlby of the Thea Foss Seaport Museum.

Credit goes to the fine photographic work by Photo Pro Imaging and Donna Gatter.

A special thank you to close friends Tom and Linda Hulst and Vicki Tart, who encouraged my writing, as did my energetic editor, Julie Albright. Norwegian community information was provided by Megan Eymann and Norm and Irma Strom; thank you for your generosity. Lastly I want to thank my wonderful wife, Kathie, who has always supported my passion for photography and tugboats.

INTRODUCTION

Andrew and Thea Foss personify the quintessential American success story. Andrew, raised on a small homestead at Skirfoss, Norway, left home at 17 to seek and eventually find his destiny at sea. Starting as a cook, he soon apprenticed and perfected his woodworking skills and spent six years as a ship's carpenter. During leave periods ashore, he visited his brother in Christiana, Norway, where he met Thea Christiansen.

Andrew decided to move to America and sent for Thea, who, being an independent young woman, waited until she earned her own passage. He chose as his destination St. Paul, Minnesota, because of the large Scandinavian population, and he began work as a carpenter building houses. Andrew and Thea were wed in 1881. The harsh winter weather did not agree with Andrew, and in 1888, he moved the family to Tacoma, Washington. Andrew changed his last name from Olesen to Fossen and then simply to Foss.

The young family made a simple float home with wood salvaged from local mills. Andrew worked as a deckhand for the Tacoma Tugboat Company and continued his carpentry to earn extra money. During a two-month trip to build a house on Henderson Bay, Andrew left Thea a small amount of spending money. She bought a rowboat for $5 from a nearby resident and cleaned and repaired it. Using green and white paint (eventually becoming famous as the Foss Company colors), she resold it for a profit. Thea continued to buy and sell rowboats, and when Andrew returned, he instantly saw an opportunity for a new venture. He started to build and sell rowboats, and with his children he created a rental business that expanded to servicing the many sailing ships that called on Tacoma harbor.

This book will show how Andrew, Thea, and their three sons—Arthur, Wedell, and Henry—expanded the company to what has now become one of the largest tugboat enterprises in the world.

Andrew and Thea would hardly believe some of Foss's far-reaching projects today. Last year, Foss crews delivered modular cargo to an international oil consortium in the Russian Far East and transported space-bound booster cores to Cape Canaveral. Andrew would recognize their still-strong commitment to Alaska but would be surprised by the massive Foss barges used to transport ore from shore to ship. They would be delighted to see Foss engineers building the first truly green hybrid tugboats to help reduce harmful emissions. Most of all, Thea and Andrew would be proud of the company's "Always Ready" legacy to customers and employees.

FOREWORD

The history of the Foss Maritime Company is the chronicle of a true American dream. It is a story of a Norwegian immigrant couple who pioneered a business in the early days of Puget Sound industry. It is a story of a small rowboat fleet growing into one of the world's premier maritime transportation companies. It is a story about hardworking people on tugs, barges, ships, docks, and on the shore supporting a growing business. The feeling of pride and shared success is embedded in the local Puget Sound culture, and the Foss family name is on roads, waterways, bridges, and a school as well as water vessels.

In 2006, we dusted off the Foss brand and launched a new logo. During the process of defining the brand strategy, employees were consistent in articulating the personality of Foss. It's not that different from the early days on the Tacoma waterfront. Foss is inventive, bold, responsive, experts, loyal, and trustworthy. I am sure that Thea and Andrew would be proud of what they created and where the company has been. These brand pillars provide a valuable balance for targeting growth while recognizing our shared heritage.

Although the Foss family no longer owns the company, employees act as if we are all shareholders. Together we celebrate the growth of the company and we share in taking responsibility for when we fall short of expectations. We operate as if Thea were still here to remind us to behave with the highest level of integrity possible.

The story of Foss commemorates a deeply rich heritage and recognizes that we are a company of caring people with honest goals and shared futures. We represent a company that is integrally tied to the local culture and with that we must act as stewards of the environment and remain community minded. We are excited that the history continues to be told and shared.

—Toby Holmes
Former Director, Marketing
Foss Maritime Company

One

ROWBOATS AND
LAUNCHES

Ole Thorvaddsen was the father of Foss founder Andrew Olesen, who was born on the family farm in Skirfoss, Norway, in 1855. Upon coming to America in 1878, Andrew changed his name to Andrew Olesen Fossen (which means "waterfall" in Norwegian) and then later to Foss. (Courtesy Tina Foss.)

Andrew married Thea Christiansen of Eidsberg, Norway, in a Lutheran church in St. Paul, Minnesota, in 1881, and they had two boys, Arthur (1885) and Wedell (1887). Andrew worked as a carpenter in Minnesota for almost eight years, but the harsh winters were hard on him, and the family decided to move to the Northwest with its milder weather. (Courtesy Tina Foss.)

In 1888, Andrew took a job with the Northern Pacific Railroad and traveled to Tacoma, Washington, which at the time was the terminus for the Northern Pacific. Tacoma proved a wise choice, as its deep harbor and wooded hills reminded him of Norway. The following year, he sent for his family, which included recently born Lillian. (Courtesy Washington State Historical Society TDF15.)

The trip west by train was extremely hard on Thea. Traveling in an immigrant train with three small children proved taxing. Only three weeks after the family was reunited in Tacoma, Thea came down with typhoid-pneumonia and almost died. While this photograph was taken in 1915, trains were still the primary mode of transportation for people coming to Tacoma. (Courtesy Tacoma Public Library.)

In this historical reenactment for the documentary *Finding Thea*, Brynn Foss Rydell plays Thea purchasing her first rowboat. The rowboat used in the 2006 film was built by Andrew and now resides in the Foss Seaport Museum in Tacoma. (Photograph by author.)

Thea reclaimed a number of rowboats and provided a good income for the family. Andrew seized on the opportunity and began to build his own boats. By 1891, the boat rental business was in full swing, and a third son, Henry, was born. The family moved the float house to a new location near the Union Pacific Railroad Bridge. Sons Arthur and Wedell helped build the float house by carrying lumber and purchasing supplies at the local hardware store. Proud of their new business, Thea painted the Foss slogan "Always Ready" on the rooftop. (Courtesy Foss Maritime.)

Supplementing the family business, young Arthur and Wedell dug worms for the many fisherman renting rowboats. The boys sold the worms for 2¢ a dozen and often earned a dime, a princely sum in those days. The Foss family c. 1893 is, from left to right, Thea holding Lillian, Arthur, Wedell, and Andrew with Henry. (Courtesy Tina Foss.)

In this early photograph, Andrew and Thea, holding Lillian on the porch, look down at a number of customers. Arthur and Wedell, even at their young ages, are helping by bailing the boats and preparing them for the next day. (Courtesy Foss Maritime.)

The early 1900s found people frequently taking launch rides or rowing boats to travel on picnics and outings. This well-attired group has packed their picnic baskets for an enjoyable Sunday outing. (Courtesy Tacoma Public Library.)

Later in life, Henry Foss told how Andrew "had a way" with boys. He allowed them to fish to their hearts' content but didn't allow any running or loud talking. The Foss family c. 1898 is, from left to right, Andrew, Arthur, Lillian, Wedell, Henry (center), and Thea. (Courtesy Foss Maritime.)

The new location proved to be a noisy one, since it was located next to the railroad tracks. One benefit was that grain accidentally dropped from the railroad cars. The children gathered it to feed the family animals, including Annie the cow. Annie was a favorite with the boat skippers, because on foggy days, she would bellow when they whistled, giving the position of the family dock. (Courtesy Tooty Foss Hager.)

Living on the water proved exciting for the family. Along with Annie the family cow, the children befriended a number of waterfront pets. Henry is shown with his pet goose. (Courtesy Tooty Foss Hager.)

By 1898, Arthur and Wedell were well-accomplished watermen. Thea purchased a 21-foot boat launch they named *Hope*, powered by a two-horsepower naphtha engine. The boys used it to deliver supplies to the ships in harbor and to rescue sailors becalmed on outings. (Courtesy Tina Foss.)

The *Hope* proved so successful that Andrew and his two brothers, Iver and Peter, began building launches as well as rowboats. The *Uncle Sam* became part of the Foss Launch Company. (Courtesy Tina Foss.)

By 1901, the Foss family was not only providing sales and rentals, but also generating services to the ships in the harbor by delivering food and acting as a water taxi for the crews. (Courtesy Foss Maritime.)

The float house at Eleventh and Dock Streets was a popular gathering place not only for renting rowboats, but also to fish for lingcod, perch, and salmon. The boys also netted for crab. In this 1898 photograph, Henry Foss can be seen waving in the small boat in the foreground. Behind him are Thea, Lillian, and Andrew (in vest and long-sleeved white shirt standing on the dock). By this time, the boathouse had become a gathering place for many Norwegians to partake of "Mother Foss" flatbread, gjestost, yulekaka, and of course, Thea's "Always Ready" coffee. (Courtesy Foss Maritime.)

Furniture items constructed by Andrew, an accomplished carpenter, include this desk built for Thea to store her business papers. It has been passed down in the family to Tooty Foss Hager, Thea's granddaughter. (Photograph by author.)

This 1904 card, listing 11 powered launches, shows Andrew and Thea had progressed well beyond the rowboat rental business. The transformation toward a tugboat company is eminent with the notation of light towing done. The map on the reverse side shows Puget Sound from Olympia all the way north to Port Townsend and the Straits of Juan de Fuca. (Courtesy Foss Maritime.)

These young gentlemen have just taken the Foss launch *Liberty* to Arletta on Henderson Bay on May 30, 1904. The *Liberty* was chartered to carry 20 young people for a supper/dance. It appears the men are collecting wood for a huge bonfire to be enjoyed that night before sailing back to Tacoma by moonlight. (Courtesy Foss Maritime.)

A group of duck hunters poses with their catch aboard the launch *Lillian D. Foss* after a day of hunting. Alongside are rowboats that were used to travel to different hunting spots or collect ducks shot over the water. The *Lillian D.* was named after Andrew and Thea's daughter. (Courtesy Foss Maritime.)

The *Lillian D.* was considered one of the best examples of Andrew's design and construction methods. After years of launch service, it became a yacht for the Foss Seattle operations. While no longer with the company, it is still in private use. (Courtesy Foss Maritime.)

On Easter morning, 1906, 15-year-old Henry Foss towed a boathouse about 8 miles from the Foss location around Point Defiance to Salmon Beach in the Tacoma Narrows. The small launch in the center of the picture with a five-horsepower, single-cylinder, two-cycle engine was used by Henry to tow the boathouse. (Courtesy Foss Maritime.)

Boat House on the Narrows

The Only Place Where Fishermen Make
a Living the Year Round
Trolling for Tyee Salmon

A New Place to Spend Your Vacation Days

For Further Particulars Call On
A. FOSS, Tacoma, Wash.
Phone Main 189

ROW BOATS Sundays and Holidays, $1;
Week Days 50c;
Per hour, 25c.
Boats stored at $1 per month.

(over)

The advertising card for Salmon Beach Boathouse, which includes a map and directions on the back, was given to fishermen. This location was chosen for its good fishing and strong eddy current, which would carry the rowboats down to Point Defiance. Andrew also chose Salmon Beach, as he had a surplus float left over from the rowboat business. The Point Defiance Streetcar Line ran a morning service as early as 5:00 a.m., which was perfect for the fisherman. (Courtesy Foss Maritime.)

In 1914, Henry married Agnes Hanson, whose family also owed a camp at Salmon Beach. While Andrew sold the launch and tug operations to his three sons in 1914, he retained the Salmon Beach operation until he passed away in 1937. Agnes's sister helped run the boathouse during the 1930s. (Courtesy Washington State Historical Society.)

By 1912, the Foss fleet had expanded to include, from left to right, the *Foss No. 8*, *Foss No. 5* (formerly the *Uncle Sam*, seen on page 16), *Foss No. 3*, *Liberty*, *Fossberg*, *La Thea*, and *Tyee*. To help with the growth, Andrew hired his brothers, Iver and Peter Foss, who had recently arrived in Tacoma. (Courtesy Foss Maritime.)

Streetcars, bicycles, and automobiles began to take their toll on the rowboat and launch business. The Foss family realized they would need to change their business practices and seek new employment for their launches. (Courtesy Tacoma Public Library.)

As these changes were taking place, the three sons, Arthur, Wedell and Henry, began to expand by towing logs for local mills. The launches were repowered, and towing winches were installed. One of the larger launches in the fleet was the "Natoma," pictured here. (Courtesy Foss Maritime.)

The *Fossberg*, a 64-foot vessel with a 100-horsepower gasoline engine, was used to help or assist vessels into and out of docks. Unfortunately the *Fossberg* collided with the passenger steamer *Tacoma* in the fog off Browns Point in 1914. (Courtesy Foss Maritime.)

The damaged *Fossberg* was loaded aboard a scow and towed back to the Foss boathouse for repairs. In 1906, to find more space for an office, shop, and living quarters, the family moved to the location pictured at 400 Dock Street. Today the location, named Thea's Park, is marked by a large stone. (Courtesy Foss Maritime.)

By 1901, the wooden sailing ships are passing, and large iron windjammers and steamships are beginning to crowd the Tacoma waterfront. The Foss family realizes that the launches are no longer adequate for assisting the large vessels, and Andrew begins to design more powerful tugboats. (Tacoma Public Library.)

Along with larger ships, huge log rafts requiring higher horsepower to tow are now appearing in many Washington harbors. This scene shows the Thea Foss Waterway in Tacoma. In the background are two bridges, one for the railroad and one for Eleventh Street. The logs are being prepared to go into a plywood plant. (Courtesy Tacoma Public Library.)

Two

TUGBOATS

While Thea ran a two-story dormitory/dining room/store for Foss employees, Andrew began to use his carpentry skills to design a pure tugboat. He worked on his own teardrop design with a rounded stern that was easy to board while working log rafts. (Courtesy Tooty Foss Hager.)

Taken in 1918, this photograph shows the Foss family transitioning from rowboats into full-sized tugboats along with the launches. In 1916, Foss purchased the *Olympian*, *Elf*, and *Echo* from the Olson Tugboat Company of Tacoma. In 1919, Andrew renamed the company Foss Launch and

Andrew designed the *Foss No. 6*, carving a model of it out of wood. It was built in Gig Harbor by Robert Crawford in 1916. The *Foss No. 6* proved a good watercraft and the prototype for many tugs to come. (Courtesy Foss Maritime.)

Tug to better reflect the emphasis on assisting ships, towing barges, and making up and towing logs to the many mills on Puget Sound. (Courtesy Foss Maritime.)

Along with Andrew, Thea, and the three boys, Thea's nephews, Fred and Charles Berg, joined the company. In this 1914 photograph taken by Arthur's wife, Ellen, Fred Berg joins Arthur, seated at the right, and an unnamed dispatcher. Notice the megaphone used to call orders to the boats. (Courtesy Washington State Historical Society No. 1998.4.6.2–Tina Foss.)

Along with changing the letterhead, Foss also began issuing yearly tide tables/calendars, a practice that continues today. The 1918 tide table listed company officers and positions as: Andrew Foss, president (repairs); Fred Berg, vice president (dispatcher); Arthur Foss, treasurer (collections, purchasing agent); and Henry O. Foss, secretary (quotations, tugs and scows). (Courtesy Foss Maritime, John Lewis.)

As the company expanded its services, the need for more space increased. The Foss operations moved to 400 Dock Street, which is known today as Thea's Park. This facility included docking floats, a store, office space, a workshop, and a dormitory and kitchen to feed and house the off-duty workboat crews. Note the *Lillian D.* with a full load of passengers in the center of the photograph. (Courtesy Washington State Historical Society.)

Not only did Andrew develop his tugboat hull with a teardrop design, which he felt resembled a fish slipstreaming through the water, but he also developed a balanced rudder that helped tugs turn in tight quarters. (Courtesy Foss Maritime.)

Although Andrew began his career on sailing ships, he was always proud of his license granted in 1897 to pilot steamships up to five tons. It covered all waters on Puget Sound within a distance of 50 miles of Tacoma. (Courtesy Foss Maritime.)

Andrew and Thea planned to send each of their children to college. Wedell earned a law degree and began a legal practice in Tacoma, in time doing all the legal work for the company. (Courtesy Tina Foss.)

In 1917, Wedell courted and married Edith Eaton of Yakima and Tacoma. Wedell and Edith had two children, Barbara and Justine. Barbara married Sidney Campbell, who played a pivotal role in the company as chairman of Foss Launch and Tug. Justine's husband, William Wood, became a vice president. (Courtesy Sandra Campbell Wright and Peter Foss Campbell.)

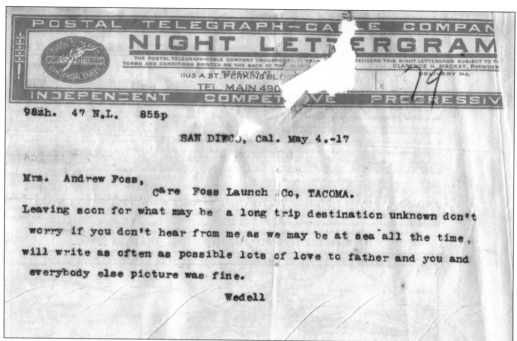

98zh. 47 N.L. 855p

SAN DIEGO, Cal. May 4.-17

Mrs. Andrew Foss,
         Care Foss Launch Co, TACOMA.

Leaving soon for what may be a long trip destination unknown don't
worry if you don't hear from me, as we may be at sea all the time,
will write as often as possible lots of love to father and you and
everybody else picture was fine.

                                        Wedell

The year 1917 turned out to be monumental for Wedell, as the Washington Naval Reserve Militia called him up for service. He joined the USS *South Dakota* (later renamed *Huron*), which sailed from Bremerton to join the *Pittsburgh, Pueblo,* and *Frederick* for patrol duty in the South Atlantic from Brazilian ports. (Courtesy Foss Maritime.)

Wedell enjoyed his time aboard the *South Dakota* and served as a navigation and gunnery officer. One of the patrols found the *South Dakota* searching for the daring German raider Graf Felix von Luckner aboard his sailing commerce raider SMS *Seeadler (Sea Eagle)*. After the war, Wedell taught navigation at the U.S. Naval Academy and retired a lieutenant commander. (Author's collection.)

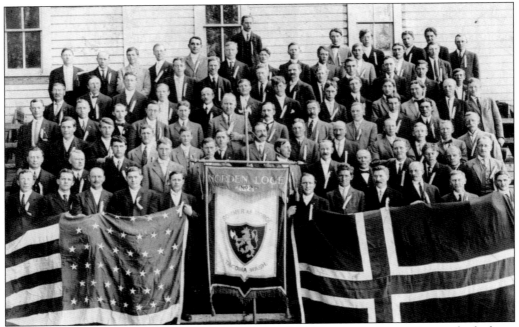

Andrew and Thea were tremendously proud of their Scandinavian heritage. Tacoma had a large Scandinavian population because its deep harbor, geography, and climate closely paralleled Norway. A gathering place for the Norwegian population was the Normana Hall located on Fifteenth and K Streets (renamed Martin Luther King Jr. Way). In this photograph, a group of Sons of Norway delegates poses outside the hall. (Courtesy of Norm and Irma Strom.)

Lena Strom (left), born in 1888, poses with two unidentified girls. Lena's husband, Sam Strom, was an insurance salesman for the Sons of Norway. He and Lena went to a number of picnics hosted by Thea and the Daughters of Norway at the Foss boathouse. (Courtesy Norm and Irma Strom.)

During World War I, the Tacoma Lodge of the Sons of Norway raised funds to buy a number of ambulances for the U.S. Army. The Sons of Norway delegation is pictured on the right after presenting an ambulance to army officials. (Courtesy Norm and Irma Strom.)

The Foss family acted as a magnet and mentor for the Norwegian community. Thea was referred to as "Mother Foss" and Andrew as "Father Foss." Not only did they provide jobs, food, and lodging for many, they also helped new immigrants become citizens. Andrew and Thea are standing in the middle of the photograph. (Courtesy Washington State Historical Museum.)

As the business grew and occupied more and more space in the floating house, Andrew and Thea moved to North Twenty-fifth and Cheyenne Streets in Tacoma. This must have been a relief to Thea, as she had always had a fear of water. In this picture, Thea, wearing a white dress, is on the right. (Courtesy Washington State Historical Society No. 1998.4.6.1.127.)

In this 1912 photograph, Thea, Andrew, and an unidentified girl are feeding the chickens. Thea always raised a large number of animals to help with feeding the crews. While Thea took care of most of the domestic animals, Andrew enjoyed raising the pigs. (Courtesy Tina Foss.)

Lillian Deborah Foss was born in 1889. While Thea loved each of her hardworking boys, she was especially fond of her blond daughter. This 1907 photograph shows Lillian on the far left in the second row of the Tacoma High School basketball team. The school was renamed Stadium High and just went through an extensive remodeling, completed in 2006. (Courtesy Tina Foss.)

Sadly Lillian's life was short. In 1914, she died of tuberculosis. Standing next to Lillian on the left is Ellen Egger Foss, wife of Arthur, who helped care for Lillian during her illness. The death of Lillian was a great blow to Thea. Lillian is buried next to her parents in the Old Tacoma Cemetery. (Courtesy of Washington Historical Society No. 1998.4.6.238.)

This Foss family portrait shows Thea and Andrew seated with, from left to right, Emma and Fred Berg, Ellen and Arthur Foss, and Agnes and Henry Foss. From the clothing worn, it appears the photograph was taken during Water Sports Day, shown below. (Courtesy Washington State Historical Society, Boland B1269.)

To honor their parents' business and commemorate Thea's purchase of her first rowboat, the boys held a water sports carnival in 1918. Included were Foss family members, friends, employees, and hundreds of community members. (Courtesy Foss Maritime.)

By the 1920s, Andrew and Thea could look proudly upon the company they had founded and watch as Arthur, Henry, and Wedell steered it into an expanding maritime firm. While their home was now located a distance from the company operations, they frequently visited to help out. (Courtesy Foss Maritime.)

In 1916, the Foss family bought three tugs, the *Elf*, *Echo*, and *Olympian*, from the Olson Tugboat Company of Tacoma. In this photograph, the *Echo* and *Olympian* share dock space with a number of World War I subchasers. The *Olympian*, to the left of the picture, was later renamed *Foss No. 16* and worked steadily for the company until November 1963. (Courtesy Washington State Historical Society, Boland A2920.)

The *Rubaiyat* was built for Capt. F. E. Lovejoy. The 65-foot vessel could haul 110 tons of cargo. The *Rubaiyat* was loaded with gypsum on August 30, 1923, when she foundered in the Tacoma harbor, suffering the loss of four lives. The Foss Company began the task of raising her from 220 feet of water in March 1924. She was rebuilt as the ferry *City of Kingston* for Sound Ferry Lines. (Courtesy Foss Maritime.)

The *Foss No. 21* started out as the *Fearless*, built and owned by the Tacoma Tug and Barge Company. In 1908, Tacoma Tug placed a wireless radio aboard her, and she became the first West Coast tug to be so equipped. In 1925, Foss bought her and gave her a major overhaul, including an air steering system and a heavy-duty tow winch. She was soon towing barges from the Quillayute River to Port Angeles. Capt. Orville Sund, her skipper, would have a long history with Foss, later becoming general manager. The *21* worked for Foss until June 1966, when she was sold to Bob Shrewsbury of Western Tugboat Company. (Courtesy Foss Maritime.)

By the early 1920s, Foss Launch and Tug, as it was now known, had expanded to Seattle, where Wedell purchased a half-interest in Rouse Towing Company. Arthur moved to Seattle as company president, and Wedell became vice president. Henry stayed in Tacoma as secretary-treasurer of combined operations. Sadly, in May 1927, Thea passed away. Her funeral was the largest Tacoma had ever seen. The tugboat fleet she had helped to found flew their flags at half-mast to honor her memory. (Courtesy Foss Maritime.)

Arthur Foss married Ellen Eggers of Tacoma. They had two daughters, Christine and Patricia. Patricia served with the company and was a member of the board of directors. Christine, or Tina, became a teacher with the Tacoma School District. Arthur bought the other half of the Rouse Towing Company and consolidated the Seattle operations. (Courtesy Tina Foss.)

The *Andrew Foss* started as a tender for coastal defense forts in California. She was purchased by Foss in March 1923. The *Andrew*, named after the company founder, became the first Foss tug to use a family name, a practice that continues to this day. She towed to British Columbia, Alaska, Oregon, and California. (Courtesy Tacoma Public Library.)

This undated photograph shows some of the crew of the *Andrew Foss*. She usually carried a captain, mate, engineer/oiler, two deckhands, and a cook. On August 4, 1951, the *Andrew Foss*, while towing the barge *Foss No. 138*, collided with the tug *Macloufay* in the Grenville Channel in British Columbia. The *Andrew* sank quickly, suffering the tragic loss of the cook. (Courtesy Foss Maritime.)

After Thea's death, Andrew continued to play a supervisory role and often visited the Foss office in Tacoma. Andrew was still plagued by illness brought on by the harsh winters in St. Paul. He passed away at 82 in 1937. (Courtesy Tina Foss.)

Andrew left behind an eloquent will that had instructions for his funeral service. He desired his sons to speak at the funeral and erect a monument on his grave that would look like the last model tug he had made. (Courtesy Tooty Foss Hager.)

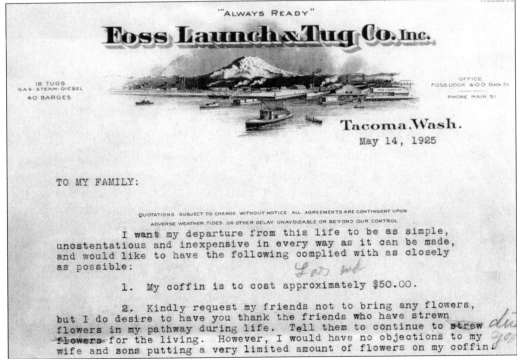

"ALWAYS READY"

Foss Launch & Tug Co. Inc.

18 TUGS
GAS-STEAM-DIESEL
40 BARGES

OFFICE
FOSS DOCK 400 Dock St.

PHONE MAIN 51

Tacoma. Wash.

May 14, 1925

TO MY FAMILY:

QUOTATIONS SUBJECT TO CHANGE WITHOUT NOTICE. ALL AGREEMENTS ARE CONTINGENT UPON
ADVERSE WEATHER, TIDES, OR OTHER DELAY UNAVOIDABLE OR BEYOND OUR CONTROL.

I want my departure from this life to be as simple, unostentatious and inexpensive in every way as it can be made, and would like to have the following complied with as closely as possible:

1. My coffin is to cost approximately $50.00.

2. Kindly request my friends not to bring any flowers, but I do desire to have you thank the friends who have strewn flowers in my pathway during life. Tell them to continue to strew flowers for the living. However, I would have no objections to my wife and sons putting a very limited amount of flowers on my coffin

Like many Foss tugs, the *Martha* originally began serving another master. She was built as a steam-powered fish packer; her homeport was in Juneau, Alaska. Foss purchased her in January 1926. She was the second tug to be named after a family member; Martha was Andrew's mother. (Courtesy Foss Maritime.)

The *Martha Foss* and *Lorna Foss* are seen moving a large wood burner used by mills to burn slash and waste wood. The *Martha* had a long history with the lumber industry towing logs from Port

On the foggy morning of May 21, 1946, on her way to Port Angeles, the *Martha* with Capt. Warren Waterman at the helm was rammed off Green Point by the steamer *Iroquois*. Practically cutting the tug in half, the *Iroquois* hit so hard she detached the pilothouse. The *Martha's* crew was able to swim away from the tug before she rolled over and sank. Unfortunately the first assistant engineer, Nelson Gillette, on watch in the engine room, was lost with the tug. In this unidentified photograph, someone has recovered the pilothouse and used it as a cabin. (Courtesy Foss Maritime.)

Angeles during World War II. During a one-year period, her logbook recorded she had towed over 775 sections of logs. (Courtesy Puget Sound Maritime Historical Society.)

Like some of her sisters, the *Foss No. 18* started service as a steam cannery-tender. Foss purchased her in 1919 and changed her name from *Alice* to *Foss No. 18*. She was repowered in 1923 and often was able to beat steam-powered tugs of similar horsepower in towing log rafts from Shelton to Tacoma. During World War II, *Foss No. 18* was transferred to the Army Transportation Service and worked in the Tacoma and Seattle harbors helping government and commercial ships in and out of berth. After the war, she was returned to Foss and worked until September 1970. (Courtesy Foss Maritime.)

While the 1930s saw a worldwide depression and a terrible recession in the economy, Foss continued to grow. The company's primary business of towing logs, wood chips, and hog fuel was supplemented by more long-distance tows. In 1933, Foss secured a contract to make regular runs to Alaska for Union Oil Company. As the tow size increased, so did the horsepower and the need for larger crews. This photograph shows the tug *Rustler* (later *Edith Foss*) with an eight-man crew just before leaving Tacoma for San Francisco and Honolulu towing three barges. (Courtesy Foss Maritime.)

The *Peggy Foss* was purchased from Ballard Hardware, Inc., for whom she had been a salmon trawler. Ironically there was no Peggy in the Foss family. *Peggy Foss*'s career was spent working within the confines of Salmon Bay and Lake Union. Thea and Andrew's great-grandson Pete Campbell remembers going with his father, Sid, on Saturdays to check boom sticks and raft ties on this tug. Later both Sid and Pete held prominent positions in the company. (Courtesy Foss Maritime.)

The new member of the Foss Co.
"The Grandson"

Length 58 ft., Width 16 ft., Draft 5 ft. Powered with 120 H. P. Fairbanks-Morse Full Diesel
Especially constructed for the particular work of the International Wood & Sulphite Co.
Towing scows over Stanwood Flats and through the Straights of Juan de Fuca.

The *Drew Foss*, like the *Foss No. 11*, was built in the Tacoma Foss yard. She was named after the son of Henry and Agnes Foss. The *Drew* worked primarily in the Tacoma harbor but often towed logs, lumber, and chip scows in the inland Puget Sound waters. Foss sold the *Drew* in 1975 and replaced her with a new 3,000-horsepower ocean tug they named the *Drew*. Several family members have been so honored when an older tug is sold and a newer one placed in service. The *Iver*, *Barbara*, *Justine*, *Henry*, *Andrew*, and *Arthur* are all third-time renamings, and the *Edith Foss* has been renamed four times. (Courtesy Foss Maritime.)

The *Foss No. 11* was constructed entirely by the Foss Company in their Tacoma shipyard. She was constructed with a heavy-duty Fairbanks-Morse engine to give her plenty of power for Tacoma harbor work and towing barges between Puget Sound ports. In 1929, Washington State began construction of a coast highway between Gray's Harbor and Port Angeles. The *11* was used to deliver barges to the Hoh River construction site. (Courtesy Foss Maritime.)

On the morning of July 13, 1929, the *Foss No. 11* ran aground at the Hoh river bar. Fortunately a crewman had a camera along and was able to record the event. (Courtesy Foss Maritime.)

While the tug encountered relatively minor damage, the crew worried about the wind and the ocean waves smashing into the tug. In this photograph, the crew has braced the tug against tipping and constructed a temporary shelter. (Courtesy Foss Maritime.)

The crew remained cool, calm, and collected while setting up temporary quarters. Unfortunately the location of the grounding was a distance from any help or communications. Later that day at high tide, the crew was able to free her from the beach. During the Second World War, the *Foss No. 11* was chartered for work in Honolulu and was freighted over on the deck of a cargo ship. (Courtesy Foss Maritime.)

By the late 1920s and 1930s, fewer sailing ships visited Tacoma and Seattle ports, and large, heavier steam cargo ships carried most of the goods into and out of port. Foss still provided launch service as well as ship-assist tugs to dock and undock. (Courtesy Tacoma Public Library.)

During the winter of 1929, the Pacific Northwest was faced with a rare occurrence—a severe drought. Most of Tacoma's power was supplied by Cushman Dam, and the drought left the water level too low to supply power. After a great deal of haggling, the navy agreed to let the city draw power from the aircraft carrier USS *Lexington*. Foss assisted navy tugs in the docking procedure. (Courtesy Foss Maritime.)

On Tuesday, December 17, the *Lexington*'s four giant generators began sending power to the city line. The *Lexington* was able to provide 20,000 kilowatts for 12 hours each day. This fulfilled about 25 percent of Tacoma's power needs and allowed City Light to store more water at Cushman Dam. (Courtesy of Tacoma Public Library.)

The *Lexington* and crew were a big hit in Tacoma. Tacoma provided a special bus route every 20 minutes to the carrier. Special holiday programs and dances were scheduled, and 70 apartments were provided for officers' families that had come to Tacoma. On January 17, 1930, with the rains back to normal, the *Lexington* left Tacoma to resume normal navy duties. Tacomans watched for news of their carrier, the "Lady Lex," and grieved when she was sunk during the Battle of the Coral Sea on May 8, 1942. (Courtesy Tacoma Public Library.)

This undated picture captures Henry Foss standing with his two children, Drew and Henrietta, who was always known as Tooty. The Henry Foss family resided at a waterfront home at Day Island. (Courtesy Foss Maritime.)

The Tacoma shipyard crew stands proudly aboard the *Henrietta* prior to her launch in 1931. She was designed by Henrietta's father, Henry Foss, and Louis Berg. The *Henrietta* was based in Tacoma and carried a captain, mate, and a deckhand who also cooked. Many Foss employees today began their careers working aboard the *Henrietta*. (Courtesy Tacoma Public Library.)

The builders added two unique features to the *Henrietta*. She was built with a 700-gallon-per-minute fire monitor, mainly used to wash off scows but handy for fighting waterfront pier fires. She also had a wraparound bumper on the stern for protection when working with barges. The *Henrietta* has been preserved in pristine condition by Mike Garvey and the Foss parent company, Saltchuk, and is often seen at maritime festivals and parades. (Courtesy Foss Maritime.)

This Fourth of July 1931 photograph shows, from left to right, the *Andrew Foss, Foss No. 21, Foss No. 18, Foss No. 16, Peter Foss, Justine Foss, Foss No. 17, Rosedale, Henrietta Foss, Rustler, Foss No. 12*, and three unidentified tugs clustered at the end. It was unusual to have so many tugs in the dock at once, and this only occurred on holidays. (Courtesy of the Drew Foss Collection.)

At 11:00 Thursday morning, June 15, 1933, the USS *Constitution*, better known as "Old Ironsides," arrived in Tacoma accompanied by her tender, the U.S. minesweeper *Grebe*. On a West Coast tour, the *Constitution* was eased into McCormick Dock by Foss tugs and greeted by Tacoma mayor M. Tennent. Old Ironsides had just come from Seattle, where her stay generated 201,422 visitors. (Courtesy Foss Maritime.)

The *Constitution* passed by the Foss office and floats and continued down City Waterway to be docked just north of the Eleventh Street Bridge. At 10:00 a.m. on Friday, visitors were permitted to board for free and view the ship until 5:00 p.m. A number of band concerts were given in the evenings to honor the *Constitution*, and her crew was given free tickets to the Temple, Rialto, Music Box, and Roxy Theaters upon presentation of their shore leave passes. (Courtesy Foss Maritime.)

The *Constitution* was visiting Tacoma as part of a nationwide tour to thank schoolchildren for donating pennies so that the famous ship could be preserved and reconstructed as a navy shrine. A large number of school tours were given, and by the time Old Ironsides sailed to Olympia, approximately 84,359 visitors had trod her decks. Illuminated by 21 huge spotlights, thousands viewed her at the dock each evening from 9:00 p.m. until midnight. (Courtesy Tacoma Public Library.)

The *Constitution*'s captain, Louis Gulliver, did have a sweetheart in every port, as his wife and three young daughters visited him at every stop during his Northwest tour. Not only did Captain Gulliver lead dignitaries aboard ship and speak at civic functions, he also took time to write a letter to Wedell Foss thanking him for the company's help in Seattle. (Courtesy Foss Maritime.)

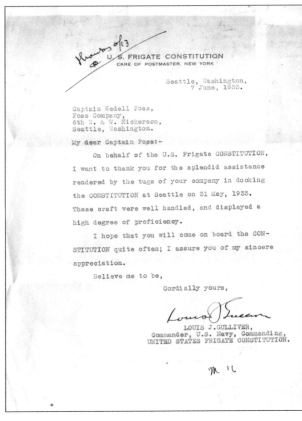

U. S. FRIGATE CONSTITUTION
CARE OF POSTMASTER, NEW YORK

Seattle, Washington,
7 June, 1933.

Captain Wedell Foss,
Foss Company,
6th W. & W. Nickerson,
Seattle, Washington.

My dear Captain Foss:-

On behalf of the U.S. Frigate CONSTITUTION, I want to thank you for the splendid assistance rendered by the tugs of your company in docking the CONSTITUTION at Seattle on 31 May, 1933. These craft were well handled, and displayed a high degree of proficiency.

I hope that you will come on board the CONSTITUTION quite often; I assure you of my sincere appreciation.

Believe me to be,

Cordially yours,

LOUIS J. GULLIVER,
Commander, U.S. Navy, Commanding,
UNITED STATES FRIGATE CONSTITUTION.

53

The *Tacoma News Tribune* reported a cookhouse fire that caused between $15,000 and $20,000 damage to the Foss building during the night of November 22, 1931. A faulty stove was blamed, and heroically, night dispatcher Capt. Bill Case was able to spread the alarm and arouse 20 Foss employees sleeping in the dormitory. Five units responded and saved some of the Foss office. (Courtesy Foss Maritime.)

This September 1943 photograph shows the rebuilt cookhouse/dormitory, parking garages, and office space, including a large concrete structure that held a safe. The ramp on the right-hand side led to floats for tying up the tugboats. (Courtesy Foss Maritime.)

To this day, Foss calendars are coveted by sailors and boatmen alike. They list the high and low tides each day and also give the time corrections for different points on Puget Sound. With the addition of photographs and paintings of Foss vessels, the calendars have proven even more popular in subsequent years. (Courtesy Drew Foss.)

During the 1920s and 1930s, the Foss brothers (from left to right), Arthur, Henry, and Wedell, expanded their towing business to include all of Puget Sound and the coast from Alaska to California. Even in the depths of the Depression, the brothers were able to add 14 tugs to their operations. (Courtesy Foss Maritime.)

The longest-lived Foss tug, the *Arthur*, built in 1889, started out as the *Wallowa*. She spent her early life towing sailing ships over the treacherous Columbia River Bar for the Oregon Railway and Navigation Company. In 1929, Foss purchased her and used her for towing log rafts. (Courtesy Foss Maritime.)

In February 1941, *Arthur* left Tacoma for Honolulu under charter to Pacific Airbase Contractors. In this photograph, she delivered a caisson to the navy in Pearl Harbor. Directly behind her is Battleship Row. In May, the *Arthur* started towing barges to Wake Island. She barely escaped by leaving Wake Island just 12 hours before its capture by the Japanese on December 23, 1941. (Courtesy 14th Naval District Photograph Collection: USS *Arizona* Memorial.)

The *Wanderer*, built for the Port Blakely Mill Company in 1890, had the distinction of being one of four steam tugs still in service for Foss when she ended her career in 1947. In 1939, she helped move the concrete pontoons for the first Lake Washington floating bridge. (Courtesy Foss Maritime.)

The *Arthur Foss* found herself on the cover of the 1936 Foss calendar. Foss was still proud of her role in the film *Tugboat Annie*, which will be covered later in the book. The *Arthur* was decommissioned by Foss in 1970 and now is owned and maintained by the Northwest Seaport Museum, Inc., on Lake Washington. (Courtesy Working Waterfront Maritime Museum.)

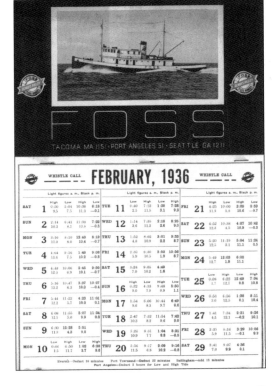

By the end of 1939, Foss was involved in another deep-sea charter to help build a naval airbase at Midway Island. The *Mathilda Foss*, with a bucket dredge, was towed by the navy ship USS *Sirius* to Midway. The trip averaged about 5 knots and took almost a month. She continued under navy contract through 1945, barging material to Midway and other South Sea islands. (Courtesy Foss Maritime.)

This December 1939 crew picture of *Mathilda Foss* was taken prior to the first leg of her South Pacific jaunt, starting in San Francisco. Orville Sund (second from left), who was to become general manager of Foss, is pictured with Henry Foss (with his foot on capstan next to Orville). (Courtesy Foss Maritime.)

The *Henrietta Foss* is towing an early Foss petroleum barge into Seattle. The close distance between tug and tow implies that the skipper has shortened his line prior to docking. Fuel barges usually carried an assortment of products, including several grades of gasoline, kerosene, and diesel. Foss started barging of petroleum products in the early 1920s. (Courtesy Foss Maritime.)

The *Dean Foss*, a twin-caterpillar, 1,200-horsepowered "D" boat, is towing the Foss barge *SEA 76*, a 12,000-barrel refined-oil barge outbound for Ketchikan and Juneau. Foss started this service for the Union Oil Company in 1930. While Alaska's cold and stormy weather sometimes made for a difficult trip, the *Dean Foss* was able to maintain a tight schedule for deliveries. (Courtesy Foss Maritime.)

The *Foss No. 100* was the first steel-hulled barge built specifically for Foss by Lake Washington Shipyard at Houghton, Washington. She was pulled north to Alaska by a number of Foss tugs, including the *Andrew Foss* and *Edith Foss*, which towed the *100* as far as the Bering Sea region, stopping at Naknek, Dillingham, and Bethel in Western Alaska. The *Foss No. 100* spent her last years on the calmer waters of San Juan Island runs, visiting Orcas, Friday, and Roche Harbors. (Courtesy Foss Maritime.)

The *Foss No. 100* is pictured on christening day, October 6, 1930, and Arthur Foss can be seen standing on the far right of the reviewing stand. Notice that the *100* has a small pump house on the stern, which had accommodations for a barge captain and deckhand/cook who stayed on the barge and were responsible for the pumping operations. (Courtesy Foss Maritime.)

In 1939, Foss launched one of its most ambitious jobs as it contracted with the Pacific Bridge Company to help build the Tacoma Narrows Bridge. This photograph shows Foss tugs maneuvering around the east-side pier. Spectators are approaching from the cement plant on the east shore. (Courtesy Foss Maritime.)

The crew of *Foss No. 12* prepared to pull the plug on an anchor barge, which would rapidly fill on one side and allow the 550-ton anchor used to hold the bridge caissons in place to slide into the water. Foss placed 48 of these 12-foot-by-51-foot anchors into the water, no easy task in current that often flowed at nine miles per hour. (Courtesy Foss Maritime.)

From various spots on the bluff, engineers watched through transits and waved flags when the barge was in position. Eight-inch wooden plugs were extracted by lines attached to the tug. The barge quickly filled and canted to one side, and the huge anchor slipped to the bottom in 120 feet of water. Foss tugs placed 48 concrete blocks in this manner. (Courtesy Foss Maritime.)

Cement was mixed ashore and poured into four large buckets aboard barges called pot scows. Quickly, the barge was towed to the bridge piers for the buckets to be lifted by crane for placement. Behind the *Henrietta Foss* on the Gig Harbor side can be seen the towers that carry electric power to Tacoma from Cushman Dam. (Courtesy Peninsula Historical Society, Bashford photograph.)

Five hard-hat divers were employed to help secure cables to anchors and inspect the piers as they were built. Often the divers worked in pairs to compensate for the strong currents. Johnny Bacon, pictured suiting up with his tenders, tragically died several years later during a dive in Pearl Harbor. (Courtesy Tacoma Public Library.)

A tender places the heavy copper helmet or "hard hat" onto the diver preparing to descend. The heavy canvas suit, helmet, shoes, and weights often weighed almost 200 pounds. The tender wears headphones and a mike to communicate with the diver. (Courtesy Tacoma Public Library.)

Even while under construction, engineers noticed that winds as low as four miles an hour caused oscillations to the bridge. Local visitors soon nicknamed the bridge "Galloping Gertie." People drove for miles to cross the undulating bridge. Toll revenues were greater than expected as people traversed several times just for the sensation of rolling while driving. Cars at times seemed to disappear while motoring across. (Courtesy Tacoma Public Library.)

Studies were conducted by University of Washington engineers, who suggested tie-down cables to help strengthen the bridge. Hydraulic buffers were added in an attempt to help control stress to the towers. (Courtesy Peninsula Historical Society.)

Lifting cranes were installed on the wire suspension cables, and prefabricated deck steel delivered by Foss barges was positioned into place. Steel workers began at each tower and worked towards the middle, riveting them into place. The solid 8-foot-high sections offered resistance to the wind and added to Galloping Gertie's problems. (Courtesy Peninsula Historical Society.)

Every stage of the construction of Galloping Gertie was considered of interest by the public. Capt. Art Wickstrom and the crew of the *Peter Foss*, which sometimes worked on bridge projects, were featured in an advertisement produced by Borden's Condensed Milk Company. Smaller tugs had limited refrigeration capacity, and Borden's touted the longevity of their products aboard vessels. (Courtesy Foss Maritime.)

Celebration for the Tacoma Narrows Bridge, the third-largest suspension span in the world, took place on July 1, 1940. Over 10,000 people attended the opening, and Gov. Clarence Martin praised the economic and military importance of the span. After the opening day, commuters paid 55¢ per car, with an additional 15¢ per extra passengers. Pedestrians were charged 15¢ to cross. (Courtesy Tacoma Public Library.)

An Official Event of Tacoma Narrows Bridge - McChord Field Celebration

DANCE! FROLIC! JUBILATE! CELEBRATE!

A FOUR - HOUR LAST FERRY - BOAT RIDE

Another Golden Jubilee on the "KALAKALA"

TUESDAY, JULY 2, 1940

LEAVE TACOMA MUNICIPAL DOCK, 8 P. M.

Sponsored by Tacoma Young Men's Business Club.

Nᵒ 757   ONE DOLLAR

From Tacoma to Bremerton via the Four Ferry Landings

LEAVING		UNLOADING AT
Tacoma Municipal Dock, 8:00 P. M.		Gig Harbor Ferry Landing.
Pt. Defiance Ferry Landing, 8:30 P. M.	Twice under the Bridge on the "KALAKALA"	Pt. Defiance Ferry Landing.
Gig Harbor Ferry Landing, 9:00 P. M.		Tacoma Municipal Dock.
Passengers Only—No Autos		Come in Costume If Possible

The Thrill of a Laughtime on the Last Ferry!

Many celebrations were held to commemorate the opening. Foot passengers were encouraged to dress formally or wear costumes for the last ferry ride between Tacoma and Gig Harbor. The famous ferry *Kalakala* was chartered, and the U.S. Army Air Force from nearby McChord Field provided an aerial exhibition. (Courtesy Tacoma Public Library.)

Fall approached, winds became stronger, and Gertie really began to gallop. On the morning of November 7, 1940, Leonard Coatsworth, a *Tacoma News Tribune* photographer, and his dog, Tubby, started across the bridge but had to stop mid-span because of the violent rolling. Coatsworth had to abandon the fearful Tubby and crawl back to the Tacoma-side tower. (Courtesy Peninsula Historical Society.)

Sadly Leonard was unable to coax Tubby from the car; the dog tumbled to his death when the bridge collapsed. Engineers from around the world studied the collapse and made many design improvements before the new bridge, nicknamed "Sturdy Gertie," was dedicated on October 14, 1950. The new bridge, at 5,979 feet, was 40 feet longer than the first bridge. (Courtesy Peninsula Historical Society.)

In 2003, Foss again became involved with the Narrows Bridge when construction of a second bridge to stand alongside was begun to help alleviate the huge amount of traffic between the Kitsap Peninsula and Tacoma. On Monday, July 21, the *Lindsey* and *Garth*, enhanced tractor tugs, aided by the *Wedell* and *Barbara Foss*, towed a gigantic 78-foot-high caisson to the south of the existing bridge. (Photograph by author.)

The massive caisson traveled the 10-mile route from the Port of Tacoma to the bridge site at approximately one and a half knots. The tugs then held the caisson in place while cables were attached to anchors that had been installed prior to the move. In the upper left corner, the *Lindsey* and *Barbara Foss* can be seen holding the caisson in position. (Photograph by author.)

Steelworkers wait to connect the first wire cables brought from the east and west towers by the *Shelley* and *Henry Foss*. The cables were joined by a metal connection called a fishplate then quickly tightened and wrapped with other wires to hold the bridge decks in place. (Photograph by author.)

The Foss tractor tug, *Pacific Explorer*, maneuvers the first bridge deck off the holding barge, *Marmac 12*, which Foss had converted to carry z-drive units. The extra drive units helped hold the barge in place against the strong Narrows tides. Compare the current deck section to the 1940 deck section shown on page 65. (Photograph by author.)

The *Mathilda*, *Henrietta*, and *Foss No. 15* take part in the April 24, 1938, Tacoma Marine Carnival organized by the Young Men's Business Club. This event at Point Defiance Park drew thousands of people to see tugboat races, air shows, and logrolling events. Just astern of the *Mathilda* can be seen the family yacht, the first *Thea*, which was later named the *Mitlite*. (Courtesy the Tacoma Public Library.)

The 1920s and 1930s saw tremendous growth at the Port of Tacoma. This photograph shows Pier 1, which welcomed its first ship, the *Edmore*, for a load of lumber on March 25, 1921. Across the Blair Waterway can be seen the top of the huge bulk storage transit shed constructed in 1923, which included a conveyor system inside and dockside railroad tracks to allow for easy transit of products to and from the port. (Courtesy Port of Tacoma Public Relations Department.)

By 1927, Tacoma supported over 50 lumber, planing, and shingle mills. The *Diamond B* and *Foss No. 17* move a lumber crane down the Hylebos Waterway. The crane may have been owned by the Dickman Company. The highly successful Dickman Mill was the last operating mill in Tacoma and operated continuously until it was destroyed by fire in 1977. Its pilings are still in view along Ruston Way. (Courtesy Tacoma Public Library.)

Lumber and wood products remain major export products of the Pacific Northwest. The miki-class tug *Martha Foss* in the photograph has retrieved its tow wire and is now lashed to the side or hip to bring the barge into the dock. Notice the mate and deckhand high above the lumber stacks watching for boat traffic. (Courtesy Foss Maritime.)

Tugboat Annie was created in the inventive mind of Norman Reilly Raine. Wedell Foss was a good friend of Raine and shared stories of the tugboat world and his mother, Thea. He was always quick to verify that the refined Thea was nothing like the raucous character Tugboat Annie. Annie appeared regularly in the *Saturday Evening Post* starting July 11, 1931. (Courtesy Foss Maritime.)

Hollywood soon capitalized on *Tugboat Annie* popularity by producing a classic 1933 film of the same name starring Marie Dressler, Wallace Beery, Robert Young, and Maureen O'Sullivan. Wedell Foss provided the *Arthur Foss* to play the part of Annie's tug, *Narcissus*. (Courtesy Foss Maritime.)

Following the popularity of *Tugboat Annie*, Hollywood released *Tugboat Annie Sails Again*. It premiered to tremendous fanfare in Tacoma on Friday, October 18, 1940. In this photograph, Tooty Foss (center) had just performed a water-ski exhibition for visiting dignitaries with her brother, Drew Foss. She stands next to Ronald Reagan aboard the *Arthur Foss*. (Courtesy Tooty Foss Hager.)

On a beautiful Puget Sound Indian summer day, a *Tugboat Annie* race was held that included 17 tugs. The race started at the Tacoma Yacht Club and ended at the Foss Dock. Fittingly, the *Arthur Foss* won the Class C race for tugs over 300 horsepower. (Courtesy Puget Sound Maritime Historical Society.)

With so many movie stars, hordes of reporters and photographers were present. The *Gallant Lady*, a local yacht still in use today, acted as a press boat. Along with the tug races, photographers filmed a carnival of water sports that awarded $100 in prizes. (Courtesy Tacoma Public Library.)

Later that day, at a dinner in the Crystal Ballroom at the Winthrop Hotel, 480 guests watched as old sailor and ship modeler N. C. Garrusi presented star Marjorie Rambeau a model of the mythical tug *Narcissus*. Later he gave gossip-columnist Hedda Hopper a model of a square-rigged ship. A smiling Wedell Foss can be seen on the far right. (Courtesy Tacoma Public Library.)

The movie stars visited the Music Box, Blue Mouse, and Roxy Theaters to meet adoring fans. Henry Foss greeted them at Ninth Street and Broadway. His words were carried live by KOMO radio, which had arranged to broadcast the ceremonies. (Courtesy Tacoma Public Library.)

After the speeches, some of the film's cast placed a plaque honoring the fabled character in the center of downtown Tacoma. From left to right are Donald Crisp, Ronald Reagan, Marjorie Rambeau, Alan Hale, and Hedda Hopper. (Courtesy Foss Maritime.)

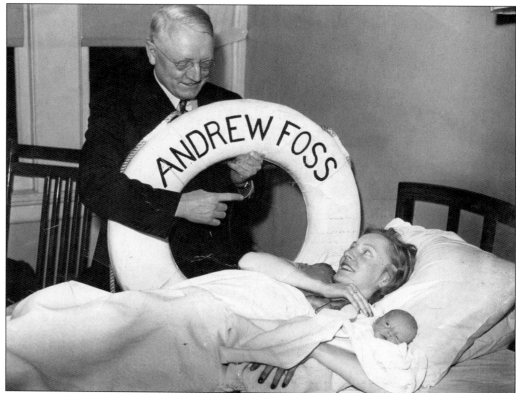

Another happy event in 1940 was the birth of Wedell's grandson Peter in Maynard Hospital in Seattle. Wedell, always keen to promote the family, is emphasizing to his daughter, Barbara, their connection to company founder, Andrew Foss. Peter grew up to have a successful history with the company, as did his father, Sid Campbell. (Courtesy Sandra Campbell Wright and Peter Foss Campbell.)

The *Justine Foss* was named for Wedell's other daughter and built at the Foss Tacoma shipyard in 1930. Her powerful 200-horsepower Atlas engine made her well suited for towing log rafts or hog fuel barges. She also spent some time in Southern California towing dump scows, and she moved north to tow the *Foss No. 11* oil barge to Ketchikan for the Union Oil Company. (Courtesy Foss Maritime.)

Henry Foss bids goodbye to Capt. Tom McInnis and the crew of the *Justine* as she prepares to leave for Wake Island to work for Pacific Naval Airbase Contractors. Later they were joined by Henry's son Drew. The *Justine* was used to transfer barges filled with supplies and materials from aboard large transport ships to the dock inside the coral-reefed lagoon. (Courtesy Foss Maritime.)

In one of the last pictures of the *Justine*, she is tied to two barges with the tug *Pioneer* and dredge *Columbia* on her right. Soon after this picture was taken, the Japanese invaded Wake Island on December 23, 1941, after heroic resistance by the marines and contractors. Drew Foss joined the captured marines and was evacuated to Japan as a prisoner of war. Tragically, later in the war, the rest of the crew was executed with 96 other contractors. (Courtesy USS *Arizona* Memorial/National Park Service.)

On August 29, 1943, Foss moved its floating office to the location of the shipyard at its present Tacoma location on the Middle Waterway. The *Foss No. 12*, *Peter Foss*, and *Joe Foss* made the move in only 31 minutes. Longtime Foss employees Oscar Rolstad, George Maddock, and Lewis Berg can be seen directing from the roof. The building housed the ship's stores on the bottom level, accounting offices in the middle, and the dispatch office and sleeping rooms and showers for the crews on the top level. (Courtesy Mark Freeman.)

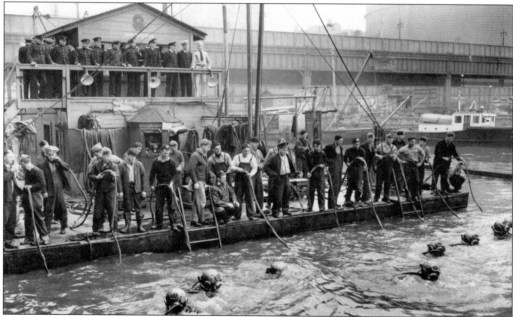

During the Second World War, Henry Foss became a U.S. Navy salvage officer serving in the Pacific. This photograph, provided by his daughter, shows him training as a hard-hat diver. It appears to be taken by the Ballard Bridge in Seattle with Harbor Patrol Vessel No. 4 on the right. Russian officers are observing from above. (Courtesy Tooty Foss Hager.)

When the war ended, Drew Foss
was evacuated from his prison camp
and transported back to Tacoma.
He met his father, Henry Foss,
returning from Honolulu aboard the
escort carrier *Takanis Bay*. It made
for a joyous homecoming when
father and son joined Agnes Foss in
their Day Island home. (Courtesy
Tacoma Public Library.)

While Henry served in the navy
during the war and retired as a rear
admiral, physical disabilities kept
Wedell (right) from active wartime
service. He did serve the war effort
ably by working with the Seattle
Port of Embarkation. Wedell passed
away at the age of 67 in January 1955.
(Courtesy Foss Maritime.)

The war found Foss tugs providing invaluable transportation services. The *Henry Foss* and Foss-owned steam tug *Wanderer* assist the C-1 cargo ship *Cape Perpetua* into the Government Locks in Ballard. An LCI landing craft can be seen astern. (Courtesy Mark Freeman.)

One of the happiest jobs Foss tugs undertook was docking troop ships returning from war service. GIs crowd the deck as the *Foss No. 16* and *Peter Foss* ease the SS *Marine Angel* into Pier 2 in Tacoma on December 12, 1945. (Courtesy Foss Maritime.)

The *Agnes Foss* was originally built for the U.S. Army as a minelayer in 1904. She was purchased by Foss in 1937 but was soon requisitioned by the navy for the duration of World War II. She was returned to Foss in 1947 and became a star of deepwater towing, going to Alaska, Hawaii, South and Central America, and even Asian ports. (Courtesy Foss Maritime.)

Famous Foss skipper Ray Quinn, noted for wearing his yellow sou'wester rain hat, oversees the connection of the *Agnes Foss* to the tow chains aboard the famous liner SS *Republic*. She had been built by the Germans in 1907, was used as a troopship in World War I, and was captured by the Allies. (Courtesy Foss Maritime.)

In March 1952, the *Agnes* and the *Donna Foss* commenced a 40-day voyage to the Panama Canal, where they transferred the *Republic* over to two Moran tugs, which took her to an East Coast yard for scrapping. The 600-foot, 20,000-ton liner yawed continuously, making it a very unpleasant voyage. (Courtesy Foss Maritime.)

The *Agnes* continued to serve Foss well for many years. She traveled often in rough seas and frequently found herself in Alaskan waters. This photograph was taken aboard the *Agnes Foss* while towing the *Marine Fox*. In heavy weather, her stern could become completely awash. (Courtesy Foss Maritime.)

Three

HISTORICAL EVENTS

By the year 1924, the Young Brothers Towing Company was engaged in transporting by barge a huge number of pineapples from plantations in Moloka'i and Lanai'io to processing plants in Honolulu. To tow bigger steel barges, Jack Young contracted the Ballard Marine Railway Company to build the *Mahoe*, powered with twin 360-horsepower Fairbanks-Morse diesel engines. The tug was designed by Seattle naval architect, L. H. "the Duke" Coolidge. (Courtesy Mark Freeman.)

Three years later, the need for more power was apparent, and Jack Young again asked Coolidge to design an even more powerful tug. So was born the "Queen Tugboat of the Pacific." The *Mikimiki* tug was launched on January 15, 1929, and sailed for Hawaii on March 30, 1929. (Courtesy Museum of History and Industry.)

When World War II began, it was apparent that the Army Transportation Service would need a large number of powerful tugs to tow barges among its far-flung Pacific outposts. The Mikimiki class filled the bill, and 61 were built, many in Washington State. The LT-142 continued after the war to work for Portland Tug and Barge and then Alaska Freight Lines. (Courtesy Robin Paterson.)

Foss Launch and Tug purchased nine Mikimikis at army surplus tug sales. They were to expand new opportunities for Foss by allowing it to operate in an ocean-wide towing mode. The Foss fleet included two twin-screw Mikimikis, the *Christine* and *Martha Foss*. Foss also owned seven single-screw Mikimikis: the *Adeline, Barbara, Donna, Justine, Leslie, Mary,* and *Patricia Foss*. (Courtesy Puget Sound Maritime Historical Society.)

The LT-376 was sold to Foss on April 12, 1946, and became the *Barbara Foss*. She could often be found towing railcar barges between Seattle and Bellingham. In 1961, she began towing lumber barges between Seattle and Hawaii. The *Barbara* spent four years on this run before towing supplies to oil-rig sites in Alaska during the late 1960s. (Courtesy Foss Maritime.)

Mikimiki in Hawaiian means "quick, nimble, fast, and efficient." While the Mikimiki was a very seaworthy design, it had a tendency to roll in heavy weather. A Mikimiki crewman once said, "They will never drown you, but they sure can beat you to death." On May 21, 1973, after long years of service to Foss, the *Barbara* was sold to Dillingham Tug and Barge in Hawaii. (Courtesy Drew Foss.)

On the foggy early morning of August 13, 1947, the Alaska Steamship Company's MS *Diamond Knot*, her holds packed with 7,407,168 cans of Alaska salmon, collided with the *Fenn Victory* outbound from Seattle by Race Rocks in the Straits of Juan de Fuca. Answering the distress calls, the *Mathilda Foss* and *Foss No. 21* started towing the *Diamond Knot* to Crescent Bay on the Olympic Peninsula. (Courtesy Puget Sound Maritime Historical Society.)

At 8:55 in the morning, the Foss crews watched as the mortally wounded *Diamond Knot* rolled over and sank in 135 feet of water. The Fireman's Insurance Company hired Foss to help salvage the lost cargo. On August 15, divers were sent down to inspect the wreck and recommend a method to recover the cargo. (Courtesy Foss Maritime.)

Divers reported back to Henry Foss and Orville Sund, manager of Foss operations, that it would not be practical to repair and raise the *Diamond Knot*. The weather in the straits would soon deteriorate, and the cans would spoil before the ship could be raised. (Courtesy Foss Maritime.)

Walter Martignoni, surveyor for Fireman's Fund, suggested a huge underwater siphon hose be sent down to suck the cans to a barge moored above the *Diamond Knot*. By September 7, Foss had moved several barges into place, and two "underwater vacuum cleaners" began hauling the one-pound cans from the bottom. (Courtesy Foss Maritime.)

Workmen tend to some of the 27 pieces of machinery crowded on the work barge. Water can be seen cascading from the receiving barge, which is nearly filled with cans and paper debris from the cartons holding the cans. A filled barge would then be towed to canneries located in Seattle, Friday Harbor, or Semiahmoo near Blaine, Washington. (Courtesy Foss Maritime.)

At the canneries, the cans were separated from the disintegrated cartons and sorted for damage. The sound cans were opened, inspected, contents transferred to a new can, and vacuum sealed. All of this took place under the watchful eyes of the U.S. Pure Food Department. (Courtesy Foss Maritime.)

Approximately 5,744,496 cans were recovered from the *Diamond Knot*'s hold. Of those, 4,179,360 were restored to be resold. In all, about 27 percent was found in spoiled condition and had to be destroyed. A small number of cans were given to Foss and reappeared under its label. (Courtesy Foss Maritime.)

As ships became bigger, increased numbers of tugs were necessary to assist them in and out of docks. Foss soon needed to upgrade to bigger more powerful tugs. The *Peter* (bow) and *Oswell* and *Drew Foss* assist the SS *Magnolia State* from Baker Dock to Shaffer Dock No. 2 on January 9, 1948. (Courtesy Foss Maritime.)

In this aerial photograph taken on May 26, 1948, the *Foss No. 17, Drew, Joe,* and *Henrietta* can be seen fighting a fire across from the Foss boathouse, machine shop, and docks. The photograph is captioned "The Wilcox Fire." The location today is occupied by the Simpson Paper Company. (Courtesy Foss Maritime.)

Four

INTO THE FUTURE

On Christmas Day, 1955, Ed Stork brought his son along to the Foss dock in Tacoma, as he had to check equipment on his tug, the *Simon Foss*. Following a long tradition, the dispatchers called in as many boats as possible so the crews could go home for the holiday. The boom on the *Iver Foss* to the left indicates it was used frequently to extricate wires from long rafts. (Author's collection.)

STORIES OF TOWBOATING
by
TOWBOAT MEN

The *Piling Busters* books were the brainchild of yachtsman Jack Shipley and were published in 1950 and 1951. They were a collection of stories, poems, cartoons, and artwork celebrating the marine world. Unfortunately they only were published twice, but in 1978, maritime historian Gordan Newell donated them to the Retired Tugboat Association, and they were reprinted. (Author's collection.)

Annually a number of marine companies, including Foss, donate prizes and host an awards banquet. Capt. Ed Stork, on the right, is presented the first-place prize, the gold cup on the table, by master-of-ceremonies Jack Shipley. (Author's collection.)

The wonderfully imaginary story by Ed Stork, "The Time We had the Wheels on the *Simon Foss*," tells of the *Simon* running up on a Model A Ford frame. Then it coasted along at lighting speed, putting together log rafts in the shallow mudflats of Shelton, Washington. (Author's collection.)

In real life, the *Simon* did spend most of her time towing logs and barges between Tacoma, Olympia, and Shelton. Cook Harvey Colt is peering out the galley door aft as the *Simon*, working with other tugs, slowly makes its way along Puget Sound. The captain and mate slept in a cabin behind the wheelhouse, but Harvey and the deckhands slept in the foc's'le up forward. (Photograph by author.)

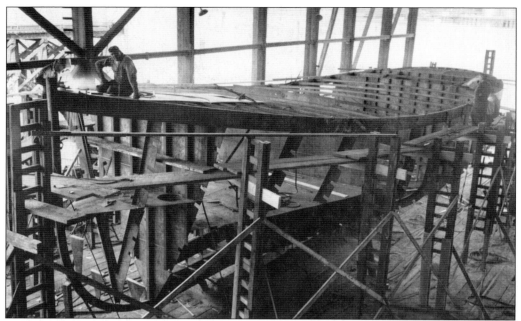

As the need for a more powerful tug became apparent in the 1950s, Foss commissioned a Seattle naval architect to draw plans for a superior harbor tug. The construction on the *Brynn Foss* was to take place at the Reliable Welding Works in Olympia, Washington. A workman is right above the steel collision bulkhead on the bow. (Courtesy Foss Maritime.)

The *Brynn*, built in 1952, had many innovative features not seen on tugboats at this time. They included electric heat and electric cooking units in the galley. The boat was originally planned to do 12-hour harbor work, with the crews sleeping off the boat, so the captain's cabin was turned into a dayroom for relaxing between jobs. (Courtesy Foss Maritime.)

The *Brynn Foss* was named after Drew and Donna Foss's newborn daughter. After the christening and launching ceremonies in Olympia, the *Brynn* was towed to Tacoma to be completed by Foss personnel. (Courtesy Foss Maritime.)

Once in Tacoma, machinists installed the *Brynn's* 800-horsepower Nordberg diesel engine. Except for the oceangoing *Henry Foss*, the *Brynn* would be the most powerful Foss tug working in Puget Sound. She would be titled the "Pride of the Tacoma Fleet." (Courtesy Foss Maritime.)

Under the watchful eye of general manager Orville Sund, machinists install the engine-room cabin and stack. The crew of the *Henrietta Foss* is standing by should they be called on to assist. (Courtesy Foss Maritime.)

The *Brynn* provided years of faithful service assisting ships, pulling barges, and shifting log rafts. She is seen passing a World War II jeep carrier, one of a number that were dismantled and scrapped in Tacoma. The *Brynn* worked until January 1978. (Courtesy Foss Maritime.)

The Mikimiki tugs are joined by the *Agnes Foss* on the left end of the group and *Wedell Foss* for the 1954 calendar. Not only did Foss buy nine Mikimikis after the war, but it also bought several war-surplus LST (Landing Ship Tank) barges that were put to good use. (Courtesy Drew Foss Collection.)

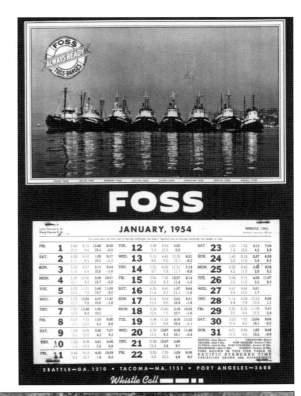

Like everything else, tugboats can experience a bad day. The *Foss No. 16* originated as the coal-burning steam tug *Olympian*, owned by Olympic Tug and Barge. When Foss purchased her, they installed a modern 200-horsepower Fairbanks-Morse engine and often made runs down the narrow channel to Shelton. The *16* ran aground in April 1954 but was quickly refloated by her crew and maintenance workers. (Courtesy Foss Maritime.)

On April 2, 1956, a Northwest Orient Airlines Stratocruiser took off from Seattle-Tacoma Airport outbound for New York. Shortly after takeoff, the pilot experienced engine trouble and attempted to fly to nearby McChord Air Force Base. Unfortunately the pilot was forced to ditch the plane near Vashon Island. A U.S. Air Force rescue plane and two boys in a rowboat were able to save all but five passengers. (Courtesy Foss Maritime.)

Foss was hired by the Civil Aeronautics Administration to raise the plane and tow it to Tacoma for investigation. The steam derrick *Foss No. 300*, which is still in use today, was used for the lift. It was found that the cause of the crash was an improper setting of the flaps by the flight engineer. (Courtesy Foss Maritime.)

Capt. Chet Elmquist is at the helm of the *Foss No. 16* on September 18, 1957. Most Puget Sound crews worked on a two-week, on/off schedule. This, of course, could vary depending on workloads. The crew typically worked six hours on, six hours off to fill the 24-hour workday of a tug. The captain could be called on watch if some particularly skillful job warranted his attention. (Courtesy Foss Maritime.)

Engineer/deckhand Ed Bishop and mate Keith McCamant wrestle a hose to the bilge pump aboard a lumber scow. Prior to the 1960s, many scows were constructed of wood and had to be pumped periodically. The pumps were kept aboard the tug and had to be loaded and unloaded from the scow—no easy job in rough weather. (Courtesy Foss Maritime.)

Deckhand Frank Burns, aboard the *Foss No. 16*, stops for lunch in September 1957. The deckhands assisted the skipper or mate on their shifts. They oiled and took care of the engine and pulled preventive maintenance when not passing lines to ships, tying up barges, and making up log tows. (Courtesy Foss Maritime.)

Cook Harold Vogel is pictured in the *Foss No. 16* galley. The cook started his 4:45 a.m. shift to cook breakfast, which would be served between 5:30 and 6:30. He would then clean up and prepare lunch to be served between 11:30 and 12:30. Many cooks would then take a short nap before preparing the evening dinner, served from 5:30 to 6:30. (Courtesy Foss Maritime.)

Young Carol Foss (right) and her sister, Leslie, daughters of Drew and Donna Foss, wave to onlookers at the launching of the *Carol Foss* in 1958. The *Carol Foss* was built at the Todd Seattle shipyard, and the Foss Seattle yard installed her single 1,200-horsepower Nordberg engine. (Courtesy Foss Maritime.)

The *Shannon*, like her sister tug *Carol*, was built by Todd in 1958. The *Shannon* was named after the daughter of Henrietta (Tooty) Foss Hager, daughter of Henry and Agnes. The powerful tugs were used mainly for ship-assist work. While no longer with Foss, they both continue in service to this day. (Courtesy Foss Maritime.)

Strong Pacific Northwest maritime tradition is celebrated each May during Maritime Week. Olympia holds a similar Harbor Fest on Labor Day weekend, and Tacoma follows with the Maritime Fest in mid-September. Each offers a chance to board Foss and other companies' tugs if the workload allows. Capt. Dan Meagher (checkered shirt) welcomes royalty aboard the pride of the Seattle fleet in 1970. (Courtesy Foss Maritime.)

Captain Meagher gives a tour of the *Carol's* engine room. A trademark of any Foss tug is its spotlessly clean engine room. Notice that Captain Meagher is holding a cleaning cloth, just in case any oil should appear before the royal pair. Today Foss often donates rides to charity fundraisers. (Courtesy Foss Maritime.)

Because many Foss tugs carry fire monitors, they are often called upon to assist during waterfront fires. On July 14, 1963, a devastating fire started in the creosoted piling of Pier 7 in Tacoma. This photograph includes, from left to right, the *Drew, Joe, Foss No. 11, Peter, Brynn, Foss No. 17*, and the Tacoma fireboat. Even with the quick reaction of the Foss boats, the damage amounted to more than $1.5 million. (Courtesy Foss Maritime.)

The Chicago, Milwaukee, and St. Paul Railroad had over 100 miles of track in two areas of Puget Sound. Since they were not contiguous, the railroad had to initiate a barge service to connect the links. Milwaukee had loading docks in Tacoma, Seattle, Bellingham, Port Townsend, and Port Angeles. Pictured is Pier 27 built along the East Waterway in Seattle. (Courtesy Foss Maritime.)

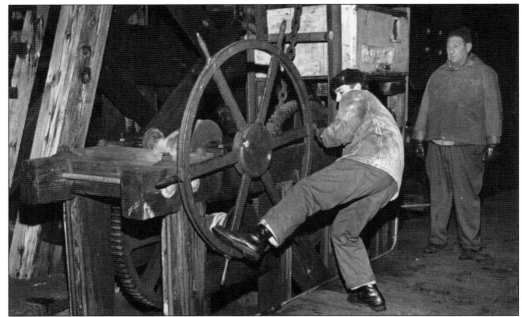

In marine operations, the tide and not the railroad timetables determined when to load and off-load. This crew is adjusting the barge to the apron prior to loading and off-loading. Each barge carried a barge captain and a deckhand. They lashed the railcars, tended towlines, and lined the barge to the dock apron. (Courtesy Foss Maritime.)

The *Donna Foss, Wanderer, Wedell Foss, Carol Foss, Erik Foss,* and *Diane Foss* were frequently employed to tow Milwaukee car floats. Here the *Donna Foss* has the barge on her hip but will drop it as she leaves the harbor, when she will attach a towline. Barges could be towed single or in tandem. (Courtesy Foss Maritime.)

The *Simon Foss* was typical of many Foss boats in that she had previous owners before becoming part of the Foss fleet. Beginning in 1897 as a passenger ferry, the *Alice*, she operated between Tacoma and North Bay. In 1902, she was acquired by the Pacific Coast and Norway Packing Company of Wrangell, Alaska, where she was converted to a tender/tug. (Courtesy Foss Maritime.)

After several more owners, the *Alice* came to Foss from the Delta V. Smyth Towing Company of Olympia in February 1941. Smyth had remodeled the *Alice*, removing the old cabin and building a one-level deckhouse. Foss upgraded the *Simon* by installing a 175-horsepower Superior diesel. (Courtesy Foss Maritime.)

By the time Ed Stork became captain in the early 1950s, the *Simon* was well entrenched in both her hog-fuel scow run from the Buchanan Mill in Olympia and towing lumber barges from the Simpson Mill in Shelton. Captain Stork was always proud of bringing five loaded barges out of narrow Hammersley Inlet in 1961, when three loads were considered a full tow. (Photograph by author.)

The author, aboard the *Iver Foss* in August 1969 with Capt. Ed Stork at the helm, waits for another Foss tug and barge to proceed from Pioneer Sand and Gravel in Steilacoom. Notice the bilge pump motor, which will be swung aboard the wood gravel barge as soon as it is tied up along the gravel loading dock, at the author's feet. The dock had wires running from each end that would pull the barge as it loaded. (Author's collection.)

The *Iver Foss*, which would later gain fame for towing the orca whale Namu, was built in 1925. She was designed by L. H. Coolidge, who eventually created the famous Mikimiki tugs. Here the *Iver Foss* is towing a chip barge past Todd Shipyard down the Duwamish Way in Seattle outbound for a paper mill in Port Townsend in 1958. (Courtesy Foss Maritime.)

This interesting aerial view taken in November 1972 shows a tremendous amount of activity at the Foss Seattle operations. The main office and docking floats are on the upper right side. The shipyard, dry dock, and maintenance building are next. Several former LSTs converted for barge work had scaffolding built on deck to accommodate modular homes being barged to Alaska. The steam crane *Foss No. 300* is working between them. In the lower part of the picture are a number of Mikimikis and other classes of tugs in lay up. (Courtesy Foss Maritime.)

A special honor was bestowed on Henry Foss, son of Andrew and Thea, in September 1973, when the Tacoma Public Schools opened a high school named in his honor. Henry and wife Agnes took an active interest in its construction. They are seen perusing the site after the developers had done the groundwork. (Courtesy Tacoma Public Schools.)

The 191,000-square-foot, $5.2-million facility was the largest school under a single roof in Washington. Henry Foss High was the first school in Washington to introduce an International Baccalaureate Diploma program. In 2001, the school was selected by the Bill and Melinda Gates Foundation as one of 16 Achiever High Schools. (Courtesy Tacoma Public Schools.)

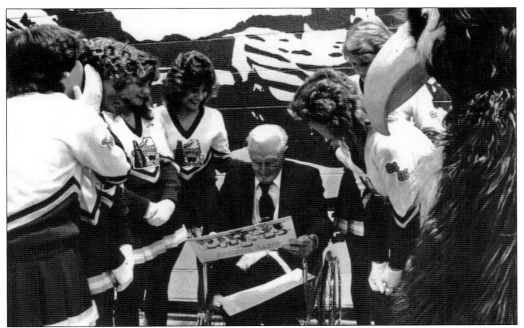

Henry was an avid school supporter. Each year, he celebrated his September 5 birthday with staff and students. They held an all-school assembly for him and shared a huge birthday cake. Each spring, he would visit when the annuals arrived to sign autographs for the students. Upon his death in 1986, the students held a memorial service for him and hung a large No. 94 Foss jersey in the gym to honor him and his age. (Courtesy Tacoma Public Schools.)

The huge ocean tug *Drew Foss*, named after Henry's son, was powered by twin EMD engines for a total of 3,000 horsepower. This class of oceangoing tug gave Foss the ability to expand its market to the East Coast, Gulf Coast, and Central and South America. In this photograph, the *Drew Foss* is towing a dredge and support barge from New Orleans, Louisiana, to Bay City, Michigan. This historic 3,750-mile tow was the first time a Foss tug had worked in the Great Lakes. (Courtesy Foss Maritime.)

In the early 1980s, Foss developed six totally new, state-of-the-art tractor tugs. They were so named because of the unusual cycloidal-propulsion system. A design committee headed by Steve Scalzo worked with Glosten Associates, a Seattle-based naval architectural firm, to develop the tugs, which were built at Tacoma Boat Building. (Courtesy Foss Maritime.)

Brynn Foss Rydell, daughter of Drew Foss, rechristens the *Brynn Foss* in 1986 in Tacoma. The tug was formerly with PacTow in California. To her left is company president Tom Van Dawark, and on her right is Don Hogue, Foss shipyard manager. A total of six of the $5-million tugs were built. (Courtesy Foss Maritime.)

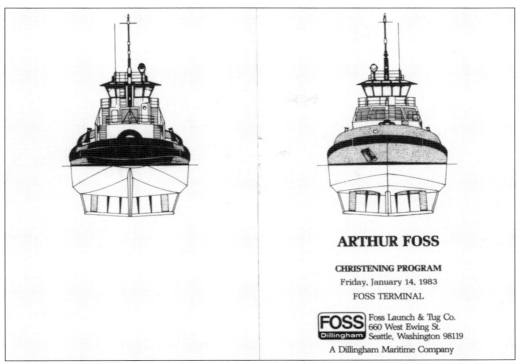

ARTHUR FOSS

CHRISTENING PROGRAM

Friday, January 14, 1983

FOSS TERMINAL

FOSS
Dillingham

Foss Launch & Tug Co.
660 West Ewing St.
Seattle, Washington 98119

A Dillingham Maritime Company

The tractor tugs incorporated the German-designed Voith-Schneider cycloidal units, which acted like eggbeaters, turning underwater blades that could change their pitch to provide excellent maneuverability. (Courtesy Tina Foss.)

Tina Foss, with her daughter Melia watching, christens the *Arthur Foss*, named after her father, in Seattle on January 14, 1983. The tractors were built to support escort of loaded tankers on Puget Sound, destined for refineries in Anacortes, Ferndale, and Tacoma. (Courtesy Tina Foss.)

While they looked almost identical, the *Andrew Foss* and *Arthur Foss* were 106 feet long with 4,000 horsepower, and the *Wedell Foss*, *Henry Foss*, *Brynn Foss*, and *Pacific Escort* were 100 feet long with 3,000 horsepower. Since 2005, several have been repowered with an additional 2,000 horsepower added. (Courtesy Foss Maritime.)

This photograph of two tractor tugs guiding the ARCO (Atlantic Richfield Company) tanker *Prudhoe Bay* through the narrow Hylebos Waterway gives one the sense of their maneuverability. Notice the stern tug is reversed and acting as a steering point and brake. (Courtesy Foss Maritime.)

Foss inaugurated its first tow to Alaska in 1922. Company founder Andrew Foss was aboard the *Foss No. 19*, which towed a newly built scow to Alaska and returned with 350,000 board feet of spruce lumber to Seattle. This photograph shows the *Claudia Foss*, which started towing for Foss Alaska Line in 1968. The *Claudia* made a round-trip run to Ketchikan, Petersburg, Juneau, Sitka, and back to Seattle via Ketchikan in a span of 10–11 days. (Courtesy Foss Maritime.)

Legendary Foss captain Jug Nolze shows one of the hazards of the Alaska run—ice! Spray would accumulate on the superstructure of the tug, and its added weight could capsize a boat. Crews had to be kept constantly on duty to smash the ice off with sledgehammers, a very unpleasant job in horrible weather. (Courtesy Foss Maritime.)

To take part in the Alaskan Cook Inlet oil industry service, Foss, in 1962, purchased two 1944-era LSMs (Landing Ship, Medium) and remodeled them into the *Alaska Constructor* and *Alaska Roughneck*. The boats were able to land cargos on beaches and carry both dry and liquid materials as well as tow in a regular towboat mode. Because of ice accumulation in Cook Inlet, they laid up in Seattle between December and March for annual refit. (Courtesy Foss Maritime.)

Another Foss project that is still ongoing is the yearly movement of lighter age barges to the Red Dog Mine operation for Cominco Alaska, Inc. Starting in 1990, the Foss team moves lead and zinc ore concentrates from shore to ships waiting in deeper water. In 1999, Foss crews transferred over 1,207,752 metric tons of concentrates from shore to 21 ships. (Courtesy Foss Maritime.)

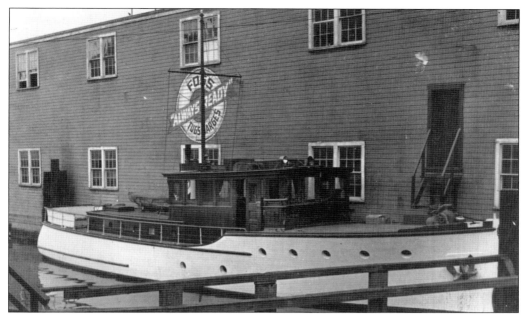

Customer service has always been a keynote of the Foss philosophy. In 1933, Henry Foss had a 54-foot yacht built that he named the *Thea* to honor his mother's reputation for welcoming people and being "Always Ready" with a cup of coffee and a warm meal. The first *Thea* was moored in Tacoma and was used until the current *Thea* was purchased in the early 1950s. The vessel, renamed the *Mitlite*, can still be seen in excellent condition at festive maritime events. (Courtesy Foss Maritime.)

To serve a large customer base, Henry, in 1950, purchased the current *Thea Foss*. Built for John Barrymore in 1930, it was named the *Infanta* after the Hollywood legend's daughter. The yacht cost over $35,000 a year to operate. Barrymore was once asked how much it cost to fuel her, and he replied, "If you have to ask, you don't own her." Barrymore encountered financial problems and was forced to turn her over to creditors in 1938. During the Second World War, she served with the navy, guarding the entrance to Puget Sound. (Courtesy Foss Maritime.)

The beautifully reconditioned *Thea* is used in the summers to entertain customers on cruises both in the Puget Sound and various British Columbia locations. She can also be seen at maritime festivals; this group enjoys Seattle's Opening Day festivities. Up to this date, the meticulously maintained yacht serves the Foss Company's owners, maritime investment group Saltchuk. The *Thea* is powered by twin Atlas diesels developing 550 horsepower with a cruising speed of 10 knots. (Courtesy Foss Maritime.)

Henry Foss sent this photograph and letter to Ed Stork in October 1968 after he had finished another season as skipper of the *Thea*. Henry hoped he had enjoyed his trips on the *Thea* "and had met many new acquaintances which is one of the virtues and attributes of a good ship." It had been typed in green ink, a trademark of Henry. (Author's collection.)

Over the years, Foss Maritime has been involved with a number of historic and noteworthy vessels. In 1983, Foss tractor tugs were asked to assist the docking of Queen Elizabeth's royal yacht, *Britannia*, in Seattle. The Queen and Prince Phillip had just visited Vancouver, Canada, to turn the first shovel of soil for the construction of Expo 1986. Foss tractor tugs were used because they could maneuver around the *Britannia* without touching her immaculate sides. (Courtesy Foss Maritime.)

Foss tugs played an important role in the construction of the Hood Canal Floating Bridge in 1960. Clockwise, from the narrow end, are the *Pacific, Leslie, Carol, Andrew,* and *Wedell.* Foss tugs were also called upon to help stabilize the storm-damaged Lake Washington Floating Bridge in Seattle on November 25, 1990. (Courtesy Foss Maritime.)

The famous Pearl Harbor veteran USS *West Virginia* (BB-48) was close to her end when this photograph was taken. She had been commissioned in 1923 and spent most of her early years with the Pacific Fleet. During the attack on Pearl Harbor, she received six torpedo hits and settled on the shallow harbor bottom. Refloated in May 1942, she continued to serve at the battles of Leyte Gulf, Iwo Jima, and Okinawa. (Courtesy Foss Maritime.)

The *West Virginia* was present at the formal surrender alongside the *Missouri* in Tokyo Bay on September 2, 1945. She was deactivated alongside her sister ship, *Colorado*, in Seattle with the Pacific Reserve Fleet. On August 24, 1959, she was sold to be scrapped in New York. Here the *Agnes Foss* and *Brynn Foss* prepare to move her from her berth. (Courtesy Foss Maritime.)

Another World War II veteran with a happier ending was the submarine USS *Bowfin*, nicknamed "The Avenger of Pearl Harbor." The *Bowfin* claimed 39 Japanese merchant ships, and four military ships sunk on nine war patrols. The photograph shows officers and crew on July 4, 1945, shortly before the end of the war. (Courtesy *Bowfin* Submarine Museum.)

In an undated photograph, the *Shannon Foss* and *Foss No. 18* move the *Bowfin* while she was still in the Seattle Reserve Fleet. In early 1972, with the help of Hawaiian senator Daniel Inouye, the *Bowfin* was transferred to Pearl Harbor, and in April 1981, she became a museum ship. She is moored next to the *Arizona* Memorial Visitors' Center and is open for tours. (Courtesy Foss Maritime.)

On March 23, 1962, former first lady of the United States Mamie Eisenhower christened the nuclear-powered cargo-passenger ship NS *Savannah*. The *Savannah* was part of the nation's Atoms for Peace Initiative. She toured many of America's port cities, including a visit to Seattle where the *Edith Foss*, *Wedell Foss*, and *Shannon Foss* assisted her into the dock. The *Savannah* carried a crew of 124 who helped with tours and was designed to accommodate 60 passengers. (Courtesy Foss Maritime.)

One of the largest ships to visit Seattle and Tacoma was the *Manhattan*. She was built in 1961 as a 951-foot-long oil tanker by the Bethlehem Steel Company. On a visit to Seattle, Foss and other towing companies provided bunkering services. In 1969, she was fitted with an ice-breaking bow and became the first commercial ship to forge her way through the pack ice of the Northwest Passage. (Courtesy Foss Maritime.)

Perhaps one of Foss's most newsworthy jobs was the towing of the captive orca whale Namu to Seattle from Namu Bay, British Columbia, in July 1965. Ted Griffin learned that the whale had been inadvertently caught in the nets of a local fisherman. Griffin built a huge wire pen to tow it the 350 miles to Seattle. The fishing boat was not able to spend the time required to bring in the tow, so Griffin gladly accepted the offer by Foss for the use of the 400-horsepower *Iver Foss*. (Courtesy Mike Skalley, Foss Maritime.)

The *Iver* and its unusual tow generated a tremendous amount of local and national publicity. The *Lorna Foss* was used as an escort boat for newspeople and a film crew. A vast crowd was on hand when the *Iver Foss* and Namu arrived on July 27, 1965. Griffin, seen feeding Namu, arranged a private marine aquarium at Pier 56. Unfortunately Namu died in his pen on July 9, 1966. (Courtesy Museum of History and Industry.)

The State of Washington, City of Tacoma, and Port of Tacoma declared June 8, 1989, Foss Maritime Day. The honor was in recognition of Foss Maritime's Centennial Year. Lt. Gov. Joel Pritchard, along with other state officials, presented Sid Campbell (right), Foss Maritime board member, a proclamation from the governor recognizing the contributions of Andrew and Thea Foss to the state. (Courtesy Sandra Campbell Wright and Peter Foss Campbell.)

Originating from a ceremonial flame in Athens, Greece, on December 4, 2001, the official Olympic torch for the 2002 Winter Olympics began a cross-country tour of the United States. Almost 12,000 torchbearers carried the torch by sled, foot, skis, and other means. When it reached Tacoma on January 23, 2002, Foss Maritime was asked to transport it across Commencement Bay to Des Moines on its way to Seattle. The *Shelley Foss* was fitted with a special Olympic cauldron and was escorted across the bay by several Foss tugs. (Photograph by author.)

In July 1969, Foss Launch and Tug became part of the Dillingham Corporation of Honolulu. During the summer of 1987, Foss was purchased by it present owner, the Seattle-based investment group Totem Resources (now named Saltchuk Resources, Inc.). While the family no longer has direct control over the day-to-day operations, Saltchuk has continued the tradition of naming tugs after family members. Foss descendents (from left to right) Tooty Foss Hager, Shannon Bauhofer, Brynn Foss Rydell, and Leslie Foss each have a tug named after them. (Photograph by author.)

Nine-year-old Lindsey Bauhofer, great-great-granddaughter of the company founders and daughter of Shannon Bauhofer (above), christened the *Lindsey Foss* on a beautiful January day in 1994 in Seattle, Washington. The string quartet from Tacoma's Foss High School played at the event, which was witnessed by over 400 guests. (Courtesy Don Wilson, Port of Seattle.)

The *Lindsey Foss* and her sister ship, *Garth Foss*, were designed for tanker escort duty in the northern Puget Sound area in conjunction with ARCO Marine and BP Oil Shipping Company. The cycloidal propulsion tugs give superior steering and braking abilities to the huge tankers now bringing petroleum products into Washington State. (Courtesy Foss Maritime.)

At 155 feet long with 8,000 horsepower, the *Garth* and *Lindsey Foss* are some of the most powerful tugboats in the world. Because of the rough weather encountered in the Straits of Juan de Fuca, the tugs were built with clipper bows and reinforced wave bulwarks, making them very dry riders. The crew of six each has their own cabin in a "floating" deck that suppresses engine-room noise. (Courtesy Foss Maritime.)

FOSS MARITIME'S NEW DOLPHIN CLASS TUG

Smart, agile, powerful and pushes things around with its nose.

The latest cutting-edge technology is the new Dolphin class tug. At only 78 feet long but packing 5,080 horsepower in twin 92 mutual stern drives, the tugs have tremendous maneuverability, which is critical in the tightly packed Long Beach, California, operations. The *Morgan Foss* was named to honor Morgan Bauhofer. (Courtesy Foss Maritime.)

The Dolphin-class tugs renewed another Foss tradition, that of the company building their own tugs. The *Morgan Foss* was built at the Foss Rainier Shipyard in Rainier, Oregon. This photograph taken August 18, 2005, shows the staff and craftsmen who helped build the *Morgan Foss*. Tony Silva (top of stairs) and Hap Richards (second from the top) were the construction supervisors on the project. (Photograph by author.)

As in the past, some Foss tugs are acquired through sales or buyouts from other companies. Emma Johnson, the daughter of Leslie Foss, christens her namesake, the *Emma Foss*. Each Foss tug proudly carries a photograph of its namesake, which Emma has just given to the crew. (Photograph by author.)

In the fall of 1989, Tacoma's City Waterway was renamed Thea Foss Waterway to honor the original location of Thea and Andrew's float house and boat operations. In 1996, Thea's Park was dedicated in a ceremony honoring the Foss family. Family members at the dedication included, from left to right, Leslie Foss, her daughter Emma (seen christening in the photograph above), Brynn Foss Rydell, and Drew Foss. In 1990, Andrew and Thea were inducted into the National Maritime Hall of Fame. (Photograph by author.)

Working in conjunction with the Working Waterfront Maritime Museum at Foss Waterway Seaport, filmmakers Nancy Haley and Lucy Ostrander produced the outstanding documentary *Finding Thea*. Here Nancy (left) and Lucy interview Tooty Foss Hager and Drew Foss aboard the tug *Henry Foss* as they reminisce about their early family recollections. The film premiered at the Washington State History Museum Theatre in Tacoma on September 11, 2006. (Photograph by author.)

While Foss Maritime is at the apex of cutting-edge technology and its business has evolved considerably from Andrew and Thea's early rowboats, the company still retains many traditions from the past. Several times a year, retired Foss tugs and their aficionados gather at different maritime festivals to honor its past. This gathering of historic tugs took place at the Seattle office on opening day of yachting season in 1989. (Courtesy Drew Foss.)

ACROSS AMERICA, PEOPLE ARE DISCOVERING
SOMETHING WONDERFUL. *THEIR HERITAGE.*

Arcadia Publishing is the leading local history publisher in the United States. With more than 3,000 titles in print and hundreds of new titles released every year, Arcadia has extensive specialized experience chronicling the history of communities and celebrating America's hidden stories, bringing to life the people, places, and events from the past. To discover the history of other communities across the nation, please visit:

www.arcadiapublishing.com

Customized search tools allow you to find regional history books about the town where you grew up, the cities where your friends and family live, the town where your parents met, or even that retirement spot you've been dreaming about.